Conquering The Mind

A Daily Devotional

Kimberly Moses

Copyright © 2017 by Kimberly Moses

All rights reserved
Rejoice Essential Publishing
P.O. BOX 512
Effingham SC 29541
www.republishing.org

All rights reserved. No part of this book may be used or reproduced by any means, graphic, electronic, or mechanical, including photocopying, recording, taping or by any information storage retrieval system without the written permission of the publisher except in the case of brief quotations embodied in critical articles and reviews.

Unless otherwise indicated, Scripture is taken from the King James Version.

Visit the author's website at www.prophetessk.org

Conquering The Mind: A Daily Devotional/ Kimberly Moses

ISBN-10: 1-946756-16-4
ISBN-13: 978-1-946756-16-9

Library of Congress Control Number: 2017961595

DEDICATION

To my Lord and Savior Jesus Christ. First John 4: 19 (KJV) says, " We love him, because he first loved us." John 3:16 (KJV) says, "For God so loved the world that He gave His only begotten Son, that whosoever believeth in Him should not perish, but have everlasting life." First Peter 3:18 (KJV) says, "For Christ also hath once suffered for sins, the just for the unjust, that He might bring us to God, being put to death in the flesh, but quickened by the Spirit."

Contents

Acknowledgments vii
Foreword viii
The Battle Within Our Minds... 1
How The Enemy Attacks Our Minds 3
Prayers For The Mind 8
Day One 12
Day Two 14
Day Three 16
Day Four 18
Day Five 20
Day Six 22
Day Seven 24
Day Eight 26
Day Nine 28
Day Ten 30
Day Eleven 32
Day Twelve 34
Day Thirteen 36
Day Fourteen 38
Day Fifteen 40

Day Sixteen 42

Day Seventeen 44

Day Eighteen 46

Day Nineteen 48

Day Twenty 50

Day Twenty One 52

Day Twenty Two 54

Day Twenty Three 56

Day Twenty Four 58

Day Twenty Five 60

Day Twenty Six 62

Day Twenty Seven 64

Day Twenty Eight 66

Day Twenty Nine 68

Day Thirty 70

Day Thirty One 72

Day Thirty Two 74

Day Thirty Three 76

Day Thirty Four 78

Day Thirty Five 80

Day Thirty Six 82

Day Thirty Seven 84

Day Thirty Eight 86

Day Thirty Nine..88

Day Forty...90

Day Forty One..92

Day Forty Two..94

Day Forty Three 96

Day Forty Four...98

Day Forty Five 100

Day Forty Six..102

Day Forty Seven...104

Day Forty Eight..106

Day Forty Nine...108

Day Fifty..110

Day Fifty One...112

Day Fifty Two...114

ACKNOWLEDGMENTS

TRON, THANKS FOR PUSHING ME TO ALWAYS BE MY BEST. THANKS TO MY PARENTS AND MY SISTERS. I LOVE YOU GUYS. THANK YOU TO EVERYONE WHO SUPPORTS THIS MINISTRY. I AM SO EXCITED ABOUT WHAT GOD IS DOING. HE HAS AMAZING PLANS FOR EACH OF US. I AM SO GLAD THAT YOU DECIDED TO INVEST IN YOURSELF SPIRITUALLY. GET READY TO GO HIGHER IN GOD.

Foreword

Conquering the Mind is a powerful book. It's filled with insight and revelation. Reading this book took me back. There were times I allowed the enemy to have his way in my mind. The enemy's tricks are only effective when he has an audience, whether it's entertaining thoughts or living according to what you see. Either way, the enemy needs your attention for his attack to work.

When I was a child, I attended a magic show in Manhattan where the magician called me to the stage. There were hundreds of people there but he chose me. As I stood on stage he put his hand behind my ear and pulled out a quarter, or so I thought. Because of my immaturity and lack of knowledge, I actually thought there were quarters behind my ear. The only reason he was able to deceive me was because I wasn't paying attention.

James 4:7 says, "...Resist the devil and he will flee." Resist means to fight against. Flee means to run away. In the kingdom we fight different than in the world. When we ignore certain things, we are actually fighting against it. When you ignore what's being said and don't entertain it, you're standing your ground and fighting against it. When the enemy does not get a response, the bible says he'll leave.

Remember, a magician needs your attention for his trick to work. After reading Conquering the Mind you will have victory in areas you didn't before. You will no longer entertain imaginations that are contrary to God. You will begin to cast those thoughts down. This book will strengthen, enlighten and encourage you.

My wife told us how the enemy warred against her mind until she resisted him. You can do the same. As you read this book daily and say these prayers, you'll see things begin to change in your life. The Lord sent you help in the form of this book. When you're done reading, share it with someone else or buy them their own copy. If it blessed you, allow it to bless others.

Tron Moses, Founder and CEO of Tron Moses' Photography
www.tronmoses.org

ONE

The Battle Within Our Minds

So many people have battles that they are fighting in their minds. They are suicidal, depressed, insecure, envious, paranoid, defeated, and the list continues. They are smiling on the outside but carrying pain in the inside. I was one of those people. I was dealing with one of the greatest battles within my mind. I will share my testimony of fear throughout this book. Everyone thought I had it all together. Many people thought my life was perfect, looking from the outside in. So many people are looking for a way to cope with their pain and stress. They turn to drugs, sex, or suicide. I decided to isolate myself and withdraw from the world.

This is where our thoughts play a significant role. Our thoughts can determine the course of our lives. For instance, if your mind is constantly focusing on success and striving for better despite being in an impoverished environment, then you would make sure that you do what you have to do in order to succeed. In other words, if you feel like you aren't going to make it, then you probably will stop trying. If you feel like you will make it one day, then chances are you will. I was the latter. I had perseverance. I didn't quit. Giving up was not an option. I was miserable in my mind. I had to fight to get my mind under control. I couldn't continue to live bound by fear.

Years ago, I was tormented in my mind with fear. No one knew it. I managed to function as I worked long hours in the hospital. People around me weren't aware of the battle that I was facing within. I knew that the key to my deliverance was changing how I thought about things. It was a process, but with God's help, my mind is no longer bound by fear. Sometimes deliverance is instantaneous, and other times it's over the course of time. All things are possible with God (Matthew 19:26).

TWO

How The Enemy Attacks Our Minds

The enemy attacks our minds with doubt, fear, unbelief, deception, and so on. He tries to plant a thought in our minds and wants us to act upon it. He will whisper all kinds of lies to you. He will say, "You are never going to make it." "Give up!" "No one cares about you." "You might as well kill yourself because you are worthless." "You will stay sick!" This is what happened to me many years ago. The devil told me every day for five years that he was going to kill me and that I was going to die. He had me believing that something bad would happen to me. I was ignorant of the wiles of the devil. 2 Corinthians 2:11 says, "Lest Satan should get an advantage of us: for we are not ignorant of his devices."

Once I recognized that everything I heard in my mind was a lie, then I was on the road to recovery. The devil is the father of all lies (John 8:44). Deceiving is what he does best. He deceived Eve in the Garden of Eden (Genesis 3:4). When I got a revelation that the word of God is true, I had to counteract the enemy's lies. Psalm 33:4 says, "For the word of the LORD is right; and all his works are done in truth." I was desperate, and nothing was working. I tried medication to get rid of the fear, and it only made things worse. So I decided to fight God's way. I began to research every scripture I could on fear. My eyes were enlightened to the truth of the gospel.

I was sitting on my couch one day, and I heard that lying voice speak again, telling me that I was going to die. That time, I did something different. I spoke back! I said, "No, I am not going to die! I shall live and declare the works of the Lord!" When I spoke, there was initially a tug of war. The lying voice tried to discourage me from speaking the word of God by saying, "Yeah right." But I decided to stand firm and not back down. I was taking back my mind! I was tired of the enemy taking over my thought life. I began to repeat and pray every scripture about fear out loud, and that lying voice stopped.

Hebrews 4:12 says, "For the word of God is quick, and powerful, and sharper than any two-edged sword, piercing even to the dividing asunder of soul and spirit, and of the joints and marrow, and is a discerner of the thoughts and intents of the heart." Every time I spoke the word of God, I was cutting the enemy with the sword of the spirit. The word of God is our biggest weapon! This is how Jesus fought and conquered the enemy in the wilderness. Every time the tempter came to tempt him, he responded with the word of God. Eventually, the devil fled (Luke 4).

God can make your mouth a weapon by speaking his word. Isaiah 49:2 says, "And he hath made my mouth like a sharp sword; in the shadow of his hand hath he hid me, and made me a polished shaft; in his quiver hath he hid me." Next, I began to practice the art of meditation. I would say a bible verse over and over again in my mind. I had a fear of being around people. How could I function working as an emergency room respiratory therapist? The emergency room is one of the busiest places in the hospital. I had to focus and meditate. My first time practicing this was supernatural. I could feel the fear coming, and immediately, I took a deep breath. Then as I meditated on various scriptures about God's peace such as Isaiah 26:3, the fear had no other choice but to leave.

My mindset was changing. But I noticed that the enemy kept trying to come back. I refused to allow him to come back, so I fought even harder. Why does the enemy try to return? Let's look at the following scriptures to gain some insight.

Matthew 12:43-45 says, "When the unclean spirit is gone out of a man, he walketh through dry places, seeking rest, and findeth none. Then he saith, I will return into my house from whence I came out; and when he is come, he findeth it empty, swept, and garnished. Then goeth he, and taketh with himself seven other spirits more wicked than himself, and they enter in and dwell there: and the last state of that man is worse than the first. Even so shall it be also unto this wicked generation."

The spirit of fear had been with me for five years. That's a long time! When I started to fight back and tell the enemy he wasn't welcome anymore, he had to leave. That spirit tried to search for another place to go but couldn't find anywhere, so he tried to return several times with seven spirits worse than himself because he considered my mind as his home. I had to replace those dry places which represent spiritual dead places with water. Jesus gives spiritual water (John 4:14). His water is life (John 4:6). Meditation on scriptures was causing an awakening within me.

This is why many people feel like things have gotten worse after their initial deliverance. The enemy is trying to get back to where he was once comfortable at. I knew that I had to take my deliverance to the next level. I couldn't keep going through the same cycle where the enemy kept trying his hardest to attack my mind. I had to fast! No food. I just had water for an extended amount of time. I did a bunch of three-day fasts. I felt so clean and pure inside of my spirit. It was the same feeling that I felt when I first got water baptized. Why fast? Some things don't come out except by prayer and fasting (Matthew 17:21)! I was getting stronger in God, and the enemy was getting weaker.

Isaiah 58:6 says, "Is not this the fast that I have chosen? To loose the bands of wickedness, to undo the heavy burdens, and to let the oppressed go free, and that ye break every yoke?" As I fasted, the yokes of the enemy were being broken. The chains of fear that the enemy once had to keep me in bondage were released! I was no longer weighed down by demonic spirits! I had the Holy Spirit living in the inside of me! I was free, and I found liberty in God's presence! 2 Corinthians 3:17 says, "Now the Lord is that Spirit: and where the Spirit of the Lord is, there is liberty." Maybe you are tired of being bound in your mind by wrong thoughts. You can also apply the same strategies I did. Prayer, meditation, and fasting will change your life, especially if you do them all at the same time.

THREE
Prayers For The Mind

I decree that I will no longer be bound in my mind in Jesus' name.

I decree that I will think thoughts that are pleasing to God in Jesus' name.

I decree that I will come to an agreement with the word of God in Jesus' name.

No longer will I accept the lies of the enemy.

I decree that I am free in Jesus Christ (2 Corinthians 3:17).

I uproot every demonic seed planted in my mind in the name of Jesus (Matthew 15:13).

I cancel every demonic assignment against my life in Jesus mighty name.

I will know the truth, and the truth will set me free (John 8:32).

Whom the son sets free is free indeed (John 8:36).

I will set my mind on the spirit which is life and peace (Romans 8:6).

I will set my mind on things above and not things on the earth (Colossians 3:2).

I will not be conformed to this world but be transformed by the renewing of my mind (Romans 12:2).

I yield my mind to God in Jesus' name.

I decree that my mind is a slave of righteousness (Romans 6:18-19).

I cast down every imagination and high thing that exalts itself against the knowledge of God, and bring into captivity every thought to the obedience of Christ (2 Corinthians 10:5).

God will keep me in perfect peace because my mind is stayed on Jesus (Isaiah 26:3).

For God has not given me a spirit of fear but of power and love and a sound mind. (2 Timothy 1:7).

I will not be anxious about anything (Philippians 4:6).

The peace of God, which passeth all understanding, shall keep my heart and mind through Christ Jesus (Philippians 4:7).

Whatsoever things are true, whatsoever things are honest, whatsoever things are just, whatsoever things are pure, whatsoever things are lovely, whatsoever things are of good report; if there be any virtue, and if there be any praise, I will think on these things (Philippians 4:7).

I decree that I have the same mind that was in Christ Jesus (Philippians 2:5).

Lord, let my thoughts be pleasing in your sight!

I decree that I will meditate on the word of God!

I will meditate on thy precepts, and have respect unto thy ways (Psalm 119:15).

I have set the Lord always before me: because he is at my right hand, I shall not be moved (Psalm 16:8).

I will submit myself therefore to God. I will resist the devil, and he will flee from me (James 4:7).

I rebuke double-mindedness in the name of Jesus.
I decree that I will believe the report of the Lord!

I decree that I will walk by faith and not by sight in Jesus' name (2 Corinthians 5:7).

I decree that the enemy will not take over my mind in the name of Jesus!

I decree that I will walk in the authority that Jesus gave me!

I have the power to tread on serpents and scorpions, and over all the power of the enemy: and nothing shall by any means hurt me (Luke 10:19).

FOUR

Day One

Today's Scripture for meditation: Ruth 1:18 says, "When she saw that she was steadfastly minded to go with her, then she left speaking unto her."

The Book of Ruth tells an amazing story of restoration. Naomi experienced significant loss when her sons and husband passed away. Yet Ruth was determined never to leave her side even though Orpah left. Ruth had a made-up mind about what she wanted to do, and nothing could change that. Have you ever had a made-up mind and nothing no one said could change it? This is how we need to be in our walk with Jesus Christ. We need to have a made-up mind to follow him no matter what we encounter.

It seems that life got harder for me when I accepted the call on my life. The enemy attacked my finances and destroyed my family at the time. Despite all the tribulations, I made up my mind to serve God with all of my heart. There were times when the enemy tempted me to get easy and fast money, but my mind was full of the word of God. I cast those evil thoughts down and placed it back on the promises of God. There is power in a mind that is made up. Remember, as your mind stays on Jesus Christ, you will not be shaken.

Dear Heavenly Father,

I exalt you. Lord, I come before you and repent of my sins. Allow my thoughts to please you. I decree and declare that I will have a made-up mind. I prophesy that since my mind is stayed on you, my faith will never be shaken. Thank you for answering this prayer. In Jesus' name. Amen.

FIVE

Day Two

Today's Scripture for meditation: 1 Samuel 2:35 says, "And I will raise me up a faithful priest, that shall do according to that which is in mine heart and in my mind: and I will build him a sure house; and he shall walk before mine anointed for ever."

Today's scripture is part of the prophecy given to Eli. God had enough of his wicked sons and the lack of honor for God. Eli honored his sons more than he honored God. The prophet gave Eli a sign that both his evil sons would die on the same day. It is important to have a faithful mind - a mind that is set on pleasing God, a mind that is set on righteous thoughts. God is looking for someone whose heart is right before him. He is tired of the injustice in the land. He has heard the cries of His people. He is raising up someone who will serve Him with his whole heart, soul, and mind. He is raising up a royal priesthood to sets standards on the earth while upholding the word of God. God is looking for someone who has the fear of the Lord in his heart and mind. He is looking for a remnant that will not compromise.

Since I started walking into purpose and destiny, I have witnessed horrific acts of iniquity in the church, people who had wrong motives and were in the ministry for the wrong reasons. It saddened my heart to know that these people did not honor or fear the Lord anymore regardless of the rebukes. They were just like the sons of Eli who the scriptures call sons of Belial (1 Sam. 2:12). Eventually, their sins got the best of them, and their ministries were no more; totally destroyed that resulted from a reprobate mind and a hard heart. I told God from day one that I will go all the way with him. I decided to be that faithful priest that God could trust to serve him with all my heart and mind regardless of what others were doing around me. Remember, just because it's popular doesn't make it right. Just because everyone else is doing it doesn't mean that God is pleased. Is your mind set on being faithful to the Lord?

Dear Heavenly Father,

I humble myself before your presence. I don't want to play any games with you. I don't want to compromise. I just want to walk uprightly before you. I decree that I will serve you with all my heart, soul, and mind. Lord, I refuse to be like the sons of Eli and dishonor you. Lord, bless my life to always bring you honor and glory. Thank you for answering this prayer. In Jesus' name. Amen.

SIX

Day Three

Today's Scripture for meditation: 1 Samuel 9:20 says, "And as for thine asses that were lost three days ago, set not thy mind on them; for they are found. And on whom is all the desire of Israel? Is it not on thee, and on all thy father's house?"

Today's scripture is taken from the story of young Saul before he was anointed King. He was very handsome, and one day, his father lost his donkeys. Saul knew that he had to seek the prophet in order to get answers about the donkey's whereabouts. As he stepped out to honor the prophet with a gift, God was lining up things for him. God didn't want him to worry because he already had the solution for the thing he was seeking. Saul was anointed by the prophet, and the whereabouts of the lost donkeys were revealed.

It is often the human nature to worry. God has spoken to me on multiple occasions telling me not to worry. Once, I bought an outfit from China and was worried that I wouldn't get it in time before I traveled out of town. God spoke to me, and I decided to trust him. I stepped out in faith and decreed what I wanted to see happen. God honored my spoken requests, and my outfit arrived in time. God is going to come through and fulfill the promises. Remember not to set your mind on the troubles but continue to honor God. As you continue to honor, trust and obey him, the solutions to your problems will manifest. Are you able to trust God regardless of what you see?

Dear Heavenly Father,

I repent of doubt and worry. I recognize that when I am not in faith, then I am in sin. I know that faith in you can cause many supernatural encounters and miracles. I decree that I will seek you and will not give up until you have granted my requests and desires. Thank you for answering this prayer in Jesus' name. Amen.

SEVEN

Day Four

Today's Scripture for meditation: 2 Kings 9:15 says, "But king Joram was returned to be healed in Jezreel of the wounds which the Syrians had given him when he fought with Hazael, king of Syria. And Jehu said, If it be your minds, then let none go forth nor escape out of the city to go to tell it in Jezreel."

Here is a story about Jehu being anointed to be King by one of the sons of the prophets. He knew the prophecies concerning Ahab and Jezebel's house. God used him to fulfill what was prophesied by the prophets. He knew that he couldn't fulfill the role of the King without the support of the people. The men around Jehu agreed for him to be King. Whenever there is agreement, then there is power to overcome obstacles and overtake the enemy. Jehu's army became bigger and his territory increased as he defeated the other kings.

Whenever we are in an uncomfortable place, we need someone to agree with us in prayer. The reason is when we can't pray for ourselves due to discouragement or distractions, that one person can cover us in prayer. We also need to have support around us as we step out and fulfill the new things God wants us to do. Two are better than one. Whenever we are down, our fellow brother or sister can lift us up. I am grateful to have a support system from family and close friends as I fulfill the call of God on my life. Just as Jehu was anointed to overtake the enemy, God will pour out such an anointing that will cause you to overcome every trial, walk in victory, and gain the support of the people.

Dear Heavenly Father,

I magnify your name. I decree that I will not give up when you take me in an unfamiliar place. I prophesy that I will overcome every hurdle in front of me. Lord, you said that you give strength to your people. Father, you said you bless your people with peace. I ask you to pour out an anointing upon me to make every demonic force coming against me flee. Lord, bring people into alignment with my destiny. Thank you in advance for granting this request. In Jesus' name. Amen.

EIGHT

Day Five

Today's Scripture for meditation: 1 Chronicles 16:15 says, "Be ye mindful always of his covenant; the word which he commanded to a thousand generations;"

The Lord will always keep and remember his agreement or covenant that He has made with you. God will always keep His promises that He made. God's word is pure and true. He has even kept the promises that He has promised our forefathers thousands of generations ago. This means that God has a blessing for you on His mind regardless of how you may feel or what you may be going through. It is our duty to always bring God back into remembrance of His word.

There were times where I felt as if God had forsaken me because of the intensity of the storms. Yet, I was wrong. I had to realize not to trust my feelings but trust the word of God. God showed me otherwise. He showed me that He was with me during the tough times. He showed me that He was mindful of His covenant. In my dry season, God gave me great promises and over time, those promises manifested. Remember, as you stay faithful to God, He will command a blessing over your life, and it will surely come to pass.

Dear Heavenly Father,

I give you praise. I am so thankful that you would choose to honor your covenant with me. You are merciful, faithful, just and so much more. Sometimes my words can't describe your greatness. I decided to have a mind that will reflect on your promises instead of anything negative. I will set my mind on you because you are the God that gives hope. Thank you for answering this prayer in Jesus's name. Amen.

NINE

Day Six

Today's Scripture for meditation: 1 Chronicles 22:7 says, "And David said to Solomon, My son, as for me, it was in my mind to build an house unto the name of the LORD my God."

King David was a worshipper and a man after God's own heart. He decided to do something great for God towards the end of his life. He wanted to build a temple for God. As he was making plans to build this marvelous place of worship, the Lord told him that he was not to build it because he was a man of war and too much blood was on his hand. The Lord told him that his son Solomon would build the temple. So, David did everything in his power to ensure that the resources and the people were on one accord to help with this task of this building.

Just as David had a plan to execute a great work for God and began to put things into place, so can you. So many people have great ideas and plans but never do anything with it. We have to commit our plans to God so He can establish it. David didn't die with the idea of building God's temple. He was able to see the beginning stages of it before he left this world. Don't die with those dreams and aspirations inside of you. Write the books, go to school, start the business, and do whatever else is in your mind. Remember to submit your works unto God and watch Him establish your plans.

Dear Heavenly Father,

I glorify your name. You are worthy of all the honor and praise. I have so many ideas and plans. Lord, I ask you to favor me and also give me favor with people. Lord, as I step out in faith, bless the right people and resources to come along so this vision that I have can be a success. I can't do this on my own Lord; I need you. Thank you for answering this prayer in Jesus' name. Amen.

TEN

Day Seven

Today's Scripture for meditation: 1 Chronicles 28:9 says, "And thou, Solomon my son, know thou the God of thy father, and serve him with a perfect heart and with a willing mind: for the LORD searcheth all hearts, and understandeth all the imaginations of the thoughts: if thou seek him, he will be found of thee; but if thou forsake him, he will cast thee off for ever."

Before King David left this world, he gave his son Solomon the instructions above which was to know God, serve him with a pure heart and an eager mind. David explained that the Lord searches the heart and understands our thoughts. He encouraged his son to seek God and find Him. He also warns him at the same time that if he forgot God, then he would be cast off forever. This is very great advice to give our children because they learn from us. Their upbringing is impacted by the things they learn at home.

Every day we need to ask God to create in us a pure heart. When we get negative or demonic thoughts we have to cast those thoughts down immediately. God is searching our hearts and trying our minds. We can't hide anything from him. It is better to deal with it in the secret place which is our prayer closets and get it right there than for God to deal with it publicly. I learned to seek God on a daily basis and instilled biblical principles into my children to seek God as well. God is looking for someone who is willing or available to serve Him and to do what He is calling them to do. Do you have a willing mind to walk in your God-ordained destiny?

Dear Heavenly Father,

I exalt you. You are all knowing. I can't flee from your presence or spirit. You know my thoughts and my innermost secrets. I just want my life to please you. Lord, always convict me when I do something that is not pleasing in your sight so I can repent immediately. Lord, keep my heart soft towards the things of the gospel. I decree that I will forever seek you and advance your kingdom. Thank you for answering this prayer in Jesus' name. Amen.

ELEVEN

Day Eight

Today's Scripture for meditation: 2 Chronicles 24:4 says, "And it came to pass after this, that Joash was minded to repair the house of the LORD."

King Joash decided to repair the house of the Lord. He was determined to complete this assignment, and he did not relent until it was finished. We have to be determined just as King Joash and complete the task before us regardless of the difficulty. He wanted to restore God's house and get rid of all the idolatry. Sometimes it takes a cleansing of our hearts, minds, and spirit man before true restoration can take place. It is up to us to decide that we will seek God and allow restoration to occur despite the trials and circumstances.

Whenever God gives me an assignment, I decide to complete that task and press through the adversity. If I feel discouraged due to lack of support initially, I still remain faithful, and over time, God will bless me with exactly what I need to have a successful project. I have to constantly renew my mind with God's word and remind myself of the awesome promises that God has made for me concerning my life. I realized that over time, nothing worth having is easy. I believe God allowed me to work harder for some things so I can appreciate it more. Make a decision to allow nothing to stop you from finishing your assignments and goals.

Dear Heavenly Father,

Lord, I magnify you. Lord, I am so grateful that you are the God of restoration. I know that you will restore my joy, peace, and everything that pertains to me as I serve you. I make a decision today to be committed unto you. Lord, use me to do great exploits for your glory. I decree that I will be faithful over the vision that you have given me. Thank you for answering this prayer in Jesus' name. Amen.

TWELVE

Day Nine

Today's Scripture for meditation: Nehemiah 4:6 says, "So built we the wall; and all the wall was joined together unto the half thereof: for the people had a mind to work."

Nehemiah had a mandate from God, and he wanted to rebuild the wall in Jerusalem. It seemed that as he went out to do what God called him to do was when the enemy did everything to stop Nehemiah from rebuilding the wall. Sanballat, Tobiah, the Amorites, and some other people threatened Nehemiah and made him feel discouraged so he would not finish the task. Yet Nehemiah had a made-up mind and he encouraged the people to finish helping him.

Whenever our minds are set out to do something, we can usually accomplish that task. For instance, when I set my mind to do an extended fast, I will not break it no matter how hungry I am. However, when my mind is not set to do something, I find myself struggling with it. There is power in the mind. We can't psych ourselves out by thinking something is more difficult than it is. Sometimes, it's mind over matter. As you renew your mind on a daily basis, you will begin to see a significant change. You will notice that little things won't bother you anymore.

Dear Heavenly Father,

I give you praise. I magnify you. Lord, I repent for thinking the wrong thoughts. Lord, I just want to please you. Lord, give me a mind to work and to complete the task. I bind up any fear or distraction in the name of Jesus. I decree that through the power and strength of God, I will overcome every obstacle and stumbling block. Thank you for answering this prayer in Jesus' name. Amen.

THIRTEEN

Day Ten

Today's Scripture for meditation: Nehemiah 9:17 says, "And refused to obey, neither were mindful of thy wonders that thou didst among them; but hardened their necks, and in their rebellion appointed a captain to return to their bondage: but thou art a God ready to pardon, gracious and merciful, slow to anger, and of great kindness, and forsookest them not."

No matter what we go through in life, we need to be mindful of God's miracles and the great things he has done before. The people in the book of Nehemiah had forgotten all about the signs and wonders that God had done. Their hearts were hard towards him, and they even rebelled against him. When we get so focused on the problems in life, we can fall into the same trap. Our hearts can grow cold against God, and we also can rebel against him. This is why it is so vital to ponder on the goodness of God and to be mindful of his promises.

When I hit rock bottom and it seemed as if none of my prayers were being answered, I wanted to walk away from the faith. However, God showed me that he was faithful. He surrounded me with his presence and eventually most of the promises he spoke to me prior began to manifest over time. God was increasing my faith in the waiting period, and I learned to trust God. I made a decision during the most trying times in my life to think of the great promises that the Lord had in store for me.

Dear Heavenly Father,

I repent for thinking negatively. I am sorry for anything that I have done that might have offended you. I decree that I will hang tight during the trying times and allow my mind to reflect on all the great things you have done. When the enemy causes thoughts of fear, unbelief and doubt, I decree that I will cast down those thoughts immediately. I prophesy over my life that I will not rebel against you but stand firm on your word. Thank you for answering this prayer in Jesus's name. Amen.

FOURTEEN

Day Eleven

Today's Scripture for meditation: Psalms 8:4 says, "What is man, that thou art mindful of him? and the son of man, that thou visitest him?"

God has set such a responsibility for mankind. God made mankind a little lower than angels and gave them dominion over all the animals on earth. We are special in God's sight. Remember God so loved the world that he sent his son to be crucified on the cross (John 3:16). Each child of God has a special place in God's heart. Their names are written on the palms of his hands (Isaiah 49:16). God has created mankind to do great things in life. Keep in mind that everyone has a purpose, but it's up to us to discover it and walk in it.

Sometimes, I am amazed at how God can use someone like me. I am a reject and have experienced some terrible things in life. Yet, the Lord gave me another chance in life. He didn't give up on me when everyone else around me did. He loved me with an everlasting love when the people who I thought would love me walked out of my life. God was mindful of me that he used me do great things for his glory! Recall, that you are loved! When you feel, no one is thinking about you or cares about you, God is.

Dear Heavenly Father,

I exalt you. I am so grateful that you take the timeout to consider me. I am so blessed to have your presence in my life. I just want to thank you for always thinking of me and loving me. I am thankful to have you comfort me in trying times. I am grateful to have you restore the lost things in my life. Thank you for your promises. I will forever embrace them. In Jesus' mighty name. Amen.

FIFTEEN

Day Twelve

Today's Scripture for meditation: Psalms 31:12 says, "I am forgotten as a dead man out of mind: I am like a broken vessel."

Have you ever been in a place of despair? You might have had all kinds of thoughts racing through your mind. You probably have been waiting for the Lord to do something for you for a long time. You might be asking God, "How long, Lord?" There is something about being in a broken place where you can find God. God is close to the brokenhearted (Psalms 34:18). Sometimes the Lord has to break us to mold us. God can use us in a powerful way at times when we are broken, meaning empty of ourselves and full of him.

Even in our broken place, God has not forgotten about us. We have to continue to pray a prayer of faith. There have been times where I was so broken that I would just weep because of the pain. It seemed that the more intense the trial became, the bigger the blessing was because I endured the storm. I remember once feeling so worthless and defeated, but I continued to praise God despite my feelings. Shortly afterward, the Lord revealed to me the reason why I had to endure the hardships. God blessed me with honor instead of shame, and he turned around the humiliating experience that I faced.

Dear Heavenly Father,

You are so faithful regardless of how I feel. Lord, I ask you to reveal the reason for the trails I am currently facing or have suffered in the past. God, give me strength and courage on a daily basis. Sometimes, my mind tells me to quit, and it feels like I am going to die and nothing will ever change, but I rebuke that in Jesus' name. I decree that you will get the glory out of my brokenness and make me whole. God, pour out an anointing upon my life for a breakthrough. Thank you for answering this prayer in Jesus' name. Amen.

SIXTEEN
Day Thirteen

Today's Scripture for meditation: Psalms 111:5 says, "He hath given meat unto them that fear him: he will ever be mindful of his covenant."

The Lord does great deeds for his people. He longs to bless them. He actually knows what's best for each and every one of us. Initially, on this journey, the Lord may have spoken to you, shown you a dream or vision, or even sent a prophet to tell you about a great promise. These are the amazing things that the Lord has in store for us or His plans for our lives. However, it seemed like those promises would never manifest because we might have gotten weary by the trials in life. When this occurs, we tend to forget about all these wonderful promises.

You may have forgotten, but God hasn't. It's up to us to still reverence the Lord despite the adversity. Whenever we honor the Lord and obey his commands, He will be ever mindful of his covenant. He will take care of us in such a magnificent way that it will defy all logic. The power of the Lord will be ever present in our lives as we place our total trust in him and abide in Him. The Lord gave me a promise that he would sustain me in the valley place and he was ever mindful of that covenant. He supplied all of my needs.

Dear Heavenly Father,

I honor you. When I think about your greatness, I can't help but smile. I am so grateful that you are my source of all things. Lord, I place my hope and trust in you. I am so thankful that you will take care of me even when I can't take care of myself. I am thankful to be able to call upon a God that is not only able but willing. I decree that I will no longer doubt the things that you said you would do. I make a conscious choice today to believe you for eternity. Thank you for answering this prayer in Jesus's name. Amen.

SEVENTEEN

Day Fourteen

Today's Scripture for meditation: Psalms 115:12 says, "The LORD hath been mindful of us: he will bless us; he will bless the house of Israel; he will bless the house of Aaron."

There are many instances where the Lord will manifest his glory on the earth because he is faithful and loyal. No matter who tries to discredit his existence, he always proves himself to be true by his presence, signs, and wonders. He will raise up mighty men and women to do a great work for him and they will be able to demonstrate his power. We have to be mindful on a daily basis that he is our helper and he will protect us from the plans of the evil one. When things around us seem to be falling apart, we have to be mindful of his promises and the covenant that he made with our forefathers.

Every day, I have to tell myself that the Lord has something greater for me than my current circumstances. He is very mindful of us. Just like the scriptures tell us that he will bless us then he surely will. I learned that there is a reason for things that are happening around me whether good or bad. I learned to ask for wisdom in all circumstances so I can pass the test and see things from the Lord's perspective. I challenge you to meditate and repeatedly say in your mind on a daily basis "The Lord is mindful of me and he will bless me." You will be amazed at how much your faith will increase.

Dear Heavenly Father,

I give you praise. I exalt you. God, I can't make it without you. Sometimes, I want to ponder on all the problems in life and analyze how you are going to fix them. Despite all the troubles, I will change my mindset. I cancel every negative thought in Jesus' name. I decree and declare that "The Lord is mindful of me and he will bless me." Thank you for answering this prayer in Jesus' name. Amen.

EIGHTEEN

Day Fifteen

Today's Scripture for meditation: Proverbs 21:27 says, "The sacrifice of the wicked is an abomination: how much more when he bringeth it with a wicked mind?"

It's amazing how people fail to realize that God is able to reveal their real motives. Wicked people may appear to do good deeds, but there could be a hidden agenda behind it. For instance, they could have a legit business to cover up sex trafficking, drugs, and other unlawful things. They could contribute tons of money to organizations as an act of sacrifice yet that doesn't mean that God is pleased with their good deeds. God is more concerned about their spiritual condition and whether or not they will receive the gift of eternal life. Great deeds won't save a person in the end, only their salvation in Jesus Christ will.

Having the right motives are important in a believer's life. Wrong motives can hinder prayers, and we will be judged accordingly (Hebrews 4:12). We need to make sure that our thoughts and hearts please the Lord. When we bless people sometimes, don't expect anything in return from them but give like you are giving unto the Lord. When you serve someone, just serve like you are serving unto God and not man. Don't serve them to make your own ministry or platform greater. Remember to check your motives because it's not about you. It's about Christ.

Dear Heavenly Father,

I give you praise. I come to your throne of grace and pour out everything that's in my heart. God, I need you to wash me in hyssop and make my sins as white as snow. Lord, I confess any ill motives I have in my heart. Forgive me. I just want to walk uprightly and do things that are pleasing in your sight. I can't hide anything from you. You are All-Powerful, and anything hidden will be revealed. Thank you for your grace and mercy in Jesus' matchless name. Amen.

NINETEEN

Day Sixteen

Today's Scripture for meditation: Proverbs 29:11 says, "A fool uttereth all his mind: but a wise man keepeth it in till afterward."

Many people struggle with holding back their words. They are like a loose cannon, and there is no filter. They speak whatever comes to their minds. They don't care if their words are offensive. They will cut you off in a conversation and over talk you. This is very foolish. Every thought is not meant to be spoken. A wise person will pause and think about the best way to deliver the message before speaking it out. A wise man will listen and process everything. If it's necessary, he might not even speak but walk away. They know that they have to pick and choose their battles.

Years ago, I was a nagging woman. I was loud, and I blurted out everything that came to mind. My words hurt a lot of people. I would comment on their hygiene, appearances, and personal business in front of them just to get my point across. I was very foolish in my choice of words. After going through much suffering, I now ask the Lord for wisdom before I speak at certain times. This is very vital for me as a prophet. I have to ask the Lord to speak through me in the best way for the person to receive the message. It works every time.

Dear Heavenly Father,

I repent of my sins. I apologize if my words every hurt anyone. I don't want to have my brothers and sisters in the faith offended at the things I say. God, give me wisdom and help me guard my mouth. Show me when is the best time to listen and show me when is the best time to speak. I decree that I am a compassionate, humble, and teachable person. I decree that I will speak words that edify others and that glorify God. Thank you for answering this prayer in Jesus' name. Amen.

TWENTY

Day Seventeen

Today's Scripture for meditation: Isaiah 17:10 says, "Because thou hast forgotten the God of thy salvation, and hast not been mindful of the rock of thy strength, therefore shalt thou plant pleasant plants, and shalt set it with strange slips."

Many times in life, when everything is going well, people tend to forget God. They don't pray as much as they prayed when they were in the midst of the tribulations or trials. They don't fast because they are content yet they fasted for many days to get a breakthrough when things were falling apart. They don't worship the Lord like they used to do when they were in a season of brokenness. There has to be a balance in our lives. Life gets busy, and oftentimes, it feels like there is not enough time in a day. But we have to prioritize our time with God.

We have to recognize that the Lord is the rock of our strength. It was through him that we held on and didn't lose our minds, commit suicide, walk away from the faith and that we had the necessities month to month when we were going through hardships. Don't make the mistake of thinking that you don't have to pray when everything appears to be going well. Don't be fooled into thinking you acquired certain things by your gifts, talents, and by your own hands while forgetting to give God his glory. There are many incidences in the Bible where people were judged due to their idolatry and they lost the finer things in life.

Dear Heavenly Father,

I magnify your name. I am so grateful that you are the source of my strength. I am grateful that I am blessed to see another day. Thank you Lord that you daily-load me with benefits. I just want to please you. I repent of the times I forgot about your faithfulness, your promises, and your goodness. I cast down every ounce of doubt, fear, and pride in Jesus' name. You are my rock, and I give you praise. Thank you for being my saving grace. Amen.

TWENTY ONE

Day Eighteen

Today's Scripture for meditation: Isaiah 26:3 says, "Thou wilt keep him in perfect peace, whose mind is stayed on thee: because he trusteth in thee."

Life gets stressful at times. We may begin to question everything. You may think, "Why Am I doing this?" "What's the purpose of this?" "I just don't understand why I am suffering," "There has to be more to life than this." These thoughts may have crossed your mind. The stressful times in life is not the time to doubt God. It is not the time to quit and walk away from the faith. However, it's the perfect time to trust God. When you focus on Jesus, you will amazingly have PERFECT peace.

I can attest to this verse. When I was going through humiliation and shame from a divorce, I wanted to die. I was devastated that the family I once knew was destroyed. I cried every chance I got, and I wanted to stay in bed all day. The reason that I was able to get dressed, go to work, and take care of my children is that I mediated on Isaiah 26:3 throughout the day. Instead of worrying about life's problems, I trusted God to heal my heart and provide for me. I can honestly say I had peace when I focused on Christ, Jesus. When I took my focus off him, I could feel that peace leave. Make a decision to place your mind on Jesus instead of the problems.

Dear Heavenly Father,

I humble myself, and I enter your courts. I know worrying never solves anything. It only causes me to get sick, depressed, and doubt you. I don't want to live my life being stressed out about things that are out of my control. Instead, I want to trust you, meditate on your word, and think about Jesus Christ. Jesus, I place my hope in you. When I abide in your presence, I find joy. Thank you for never giving up on me. I love you. Amen.

TWENTY TWO

Day Nineteen

Today's Scripture for meditation: Isaiah 46:8 says, "Remember this, and shew yourselves men: bring it again to mind, O ye transgressors."

Many people have created idols in their hearts and minds. They might not have physically worshipped and bowed down to idols, but they have placed people and things before God. God raised up so many prophets to cry out against the people's idolatry. The hearts of the people were hardened, and they forgot about the great things the Lord has done. The people faced judgment, and then they turned back unto the Lord. Don't let judgment or trying circumstances be the only reason you begin to live for the Lord. Make a sacrifice and live for God when things seem to be going well.

The enemy wants people to be blind to the truth of the gospel. He wants to destroy people in their sins. He doesn't show the person the consequences when they are having a great time fulfilling the lust of their flesh. We can look at the downfalls of the people who practiced idolatry and the price they paid in the scriptures. The enemy wants to deceive the people into thinking that their idols in their lives are the source of their blessing and their ultimate fulfillment. However, God is that source. This is why it is vital to ask the Lord to establish a real connection between you and him so you will be less likely to seek another deity.

Dear Heavenly Father,

I repent of my sins and the sins of my forefathers. God, I stand in the gap, and I repent on behalf of my nation. God, some people have tried to shut the door to you in public places and bring in false gods. Lord, cover my family, friends, ministry, and everything pertaining to me in the blood of Jesus. I renounce every demonic seed planted of false religion in my heart and mind. Lord, bless me to grow in the knowledge of your truth and glory. Thank you so much for setting me free in Jesus' name. Amen.

TWENTY THREE

Day Twenty

Today's Scripture for meditation: Isaiah 65:17 says, "For, behold, I create new heavens and a new earth: and the former shall not be remembered, nor come into mind."

God can do a new thing in our lives to the point where our past is unrecognizable. You may have been a fornicator, drug dealer, prostitute, thief, etc. in the past but now you are a minister of fire! You are a child of the Most High God. God can change the direction of your life where the plans you had got interrupted by him. In this case, God will place the burden upon you to do the things he is calling you to do. He will reroute you and close doors to lead you on the path that he has for you.

God always does new things. To walk into these things and to access them, we have to be ready to embrace them. We can't keep reflecting on the past. We can't keep looking backwards by holding on to people and things that God requires us to let go. We have to change our mindset and hope toward the future. When we do this, we won't constantly dwell on the former things but look forward to the things to come.

Dear Heavenly Father,

I exalt you. I give you all the glory, honor, and praise. I am looking forward to the new things that you will do in my life. I give you thanks for doing something new in my life. I am so thankful that you have given my life purpose. I honor you for taking my life that was once meaningless and transforming it into a meaningful life. God, I am forever indebted to you. I ask you to keep my mind stayed on you. Thank you. In Jesus' name. Amen.

TWENTY FOUR

Day Twenty One

Today's Scripture for meditation: Lamentations 3:21 says, "This I recall to my mind, therefore have I hope."

Have you ever cried out to the Lord and asked, "Why do I have to suffer?" "Why am I going through this?" "Lord, I have been praying, and nothing is happening." Sometimes, we have to suffer in life, especially if we desire to live a godly life (2 Timothy 3:12). We will face persecution, rejection, loneliness, slander, and the list goes on and on. The prophet Jeremiah suffered a lot. He often felt that God was ignoring his prayers and it saddened him. Yet, he recalled all the faithfulness of God and immediately, hope arose in him.

We have to reflect on God's sovereignty during our times of suffering. I often felt like Jeremiah when he felt God wasn't hearing his prayers. However, I had to push my feelings away and stand on the word. I had to pray out the word, and I found scriptures that told me that God hears the prayers of the righteous (Ps. 34:17, Exodus 14:10, 1 Kings 9:3, Ps. 34:4;6). Eventually, the suffering ended, and I walked into a season of restoration. I finally had joy.

Dear Heavenly Father,

I humble myself. I magnify you. I repent of my sins, and I ask you for forgiveness. I decree that whenever I feel like weeping, I will reflect on your greatness. Lord, you are more powerful than any tribulation. Lord, you are stronger. I am so glad that I find my strength in you. I decree that I will renew my mind. Thank you for your faithfulness. In Jesus' name. Amen.

TWENTY FIVE

Day Twenty Two

Today's Scripture for meditation: Matthew 22:37 says, "Jesus said unto him, thou shalt love the Lord thy God with all thy heart, and with all thy soul, and with all thy mind."

We know God is love, according to the scriptures. We are also commanded to love all throughout the word of God. We are told to not only love God but each other. Jesus basically told his followers to love him with everything they have within them. God wants our heart and our time. He wants us to trust him over everyone and everything else. He wants us to walk with him as we follow him. In order to accomplish this, we must have our minds made up to endure until the end.

I had to pray that God would prove himself to be real in my life. At first, it was challenging to love someone I couldn't see or feel, but one day, I encountered God's love and presence. The Lord proved that he was real by placing his fire on my life. He did some things that were unexplainable such as allowing me to witness the supernatural and to be a partaker of miracles. He healed my heart when I was wounded by the storms in this life. He always set me free when I was in bondage from the enemy.

Dear Heavenly Father,

I humble myself. No matter how things go in life, I need you. God, I want you with every fiber of my being. I decree Matthew 22:37 in my life that I will love the Lord thy God with all my heart, with all my soul, and with all my mind. Lord, I never want to grieve your spirit with insecurities. I never want to hurt you or let you down. Lord, strengthen my relationship with you. Thank you for your loving kindness in Jesus' name. Amen.

TWENTY SIX
Day Twenty Three

Today's Scripture for meditation: Luke 12:29 says, "And seek not ye what ye shall eat, or what ye shall drink, neither be ye of doubtful mind."

Many times, we get frustrated and overwhelmed by the cares of this world. We allow doubt and fear to set in. We are concerned with everything else except for the will of God for our lives. This is a very dangerous place to be at. When we are supposed to be spending time with the Lord, we get caught up in thinking about all types of things such as "What are we going to eat for dinner?" "What is so and so doing?" What am I going to do today?" Our minds will begin to grow carnal and our hearts dim towards the gospel. We will begin to doubt the promises of God and lose interest of his fellowship.

We have to make a choice to keep the fire of God burning continually in our lives. We have to seek God often and reverence His presence. We have to learn how to commune with the Holy Spirit. We have to build ourselves up spiritual by prayer, fasting, meditation, the study of the scriptures, and worship. We have to always be mindful of how wonderful the Lord truly is. Everyone gets tested, yet the Lord will give you strength to make it if you stay abided in Him. What's on your mind as you go before the Lord in prayer? Let it all go by trusting God to take care of all your needs.

Dear Heavenly Father,

I magnify you. I exalt you. I repent for coming to prayer distracted and not seeking you with my whole heart. Lord, bless me to always prioritize our time together. I just want to please you, and I never want to grieve your Holy Spirit. You truly are great, and you are the God that does the impossible. I am grateful that you are all-knowing. You know my needs before I even come to ask you. Thank you in advance for working all things out for me. Thank you for being all powerful. I will forever praise you. I seal this prayer in Jesus mighty name. Amen.

TWENTY SEVEN

Day Twenty Four

Today's Scripture for meditation: Romans 1:28 says, "And even as they did not like to retain God in their knowledge, God gave them over to a reprobate mind, to do those things which are not convenient."

Having a reprobate mind is a mind that is corrupt or one that is depraved. A reprobate mind is one that is set on evil. People with this mindset neglect the things of God. They feel God's ways are unimportant and they rather do things that gratify their lustful flesh. We have to be cautious to allow the word of God to run deeply in our hearts and minds. We can't allow our minds to be filled with evil. Instead, we need to make sure that we are increasing in the knowledge of God by taking the necessary steps for growth.

As I walk with the Lord, my sensitivity to his presence rises. I lose desires to do sinful things and long to do things that are pleasing to God. When the enemy plants an evil seed in my mind such as wrong thoughts or demonic ideas, I rebuke it immediately and cast it down. I realize everything starts with a seed and I refuse to allow those seeds to blossom. People with reprobate minds didn't protect their minds from evil and eventually gave in to their lustful desires.

Dear Heavenly Father,

I honor you. I want to glorify you with my life. I humble myself, and I repent for all of my sins. Lord, bless me to always be aware of your presence. I pray you give me a desire to live holy and righteously before you. Lord, draw me nigh to you and give me a burden for the things you care about. I decree that I will never be given over to a reprobate mind. I decree and declare in my mind that it will not be taken over by the enemy. Thank you for answering this prayer in Jesus' name. Amen.

TWENTY EIGHT

Day Twenty Five

Today's Scriptures for meditation: Romans 7:22-25 says, "For I delight in the law of God after the inward man: But I see another law in my members, warring against the law of my mind, and bringing me into captivity to the law of sin which is in my members. O wretched man that I am! who shall deliver me from the body of this death? I thank God through Jesus Christ our Lord. So then with the mind I myself serve the law of God; but with the flesh the law of sin."

Apostle Paul had an internal war going on. He had the word of God in his mind and strived to live right. Yet, his flesh wanted to do things that were unpleasing to God. Does this sound like something you struggled with before? I think this happens to all of us if we were to be completely honest. No matter how anointed you may be or how holy you live, we still get tempted. This is why we have to fast and pray. We also have to use wisdom and discernment in our walk.

The more time I spend with God, the less I desire other things. I often pray for a burden of intercession and a hunger for the word of God. As I read the word of God, it comes alive to me because I can immediately feel the presence of God. Whenever I get tempted and tried, I have learned to withdraw myself from the crowd and go to a quiet place to seek God. As I rest in His presence, supernatural deliverance comes through for me. Remember to allow the word of God to rule in you richly.

Dear Heavenly Father,

You are all powerful. I need you, and I want to go higher in you. I want to live holy as you are Holy. Lord, give me strength and allow me to always walk uprightly before you. Lord, bless my thoughts to dwell and delight on your word. Allow me to practice what I preach. I declare that I will yield all my members as slaves of righteousness for your glory. Thank you for answering this prayer in Jesus' name. Amen.

TWENTY NINE

Day Twenty Six

Today's Scriptures for meditation: Romans 8:5-7 says, "For they that are after the flesh do mind the things of the flesh; but they that are after the Spirit the things of the Spirit. For to be carnally minded is death; but to be spiritually minded is life and peace. Because the carnal mind is enmity against God: for it is not subject to the law of God, neither indeed can be."

Did you know that a worldly mind is hostile to God? When we dwell on things that grieve the Holy Spirit, we can backslide by sinning against the Lord. We can start to be carnal where we are doing the same thing the unbelievers are doing. For instance, we are listening to the same type of music they listen to. We are wearing the same type of clothing they are wearing. We are watching the same shows on television that they are watching. We are even acting like them, and people on the outside can't tell us apart from the unbeliever. This is sad, but it happens all the time.

People start off on fire for God but end up converting back to their old ways because they didn't take the necessary steps to live right. These steps could include disconnecting from certain people and studying the bible. The scriptures warn us that the carnal mind is death and will lead to destruction. Contrarily, a spirit-filled mind is one of peace that leads to eternal life with Christ Jesus. We need to be friends with God and not his enemy. Don't worry about being popular or trying to fit in with the crowd. I discovered a long time ago that I would never fit in. God ordained me to stick out like a sore thumb for his glory. Make a decision to be a leader and not a follower. Make a lasting impact on the people around you for God's glory.

Dear Heavenly Father,

I want to please you. I repent of my carnality. I want to uphold your standard and never try to justify my sins. I am sorry for the times that I grieved you. I ask you for forgiveness. I cover my mind with the blood of Jesus. Lord, do a work in me. I pray that you transform me into the image of your son Jesus. Lord, put to death any wicked desire within my flesh. I want to grow in you. I want to be your best friend. Thank you so much for graciously inclining to my prayers. I ask all this and more in Jesus' name. Amen.

THIRTY

Day Twenty Seven

Today's Scripture for meditation: Romans 8:27 says, "And he that searcheth the hearts knoweth what is the mind of the Spirit because he maketh intercession for the saints according to the will of God."

Have you ever pondered how much the spirit of God makes intercession for us? It's amazing how we can pray in our heavenly language during the toughest times in life. We can pray a perfect prayer of faith by praying in tongues. The Holy Spirit is praying for the will of God to be done in our lives. When we might feel like we have run out of words to pray, praying in tongues is necessary. The Holy Spirit is your friend. Allow him to pray for you.

During the most difficult season of my life, I found myself praying in tongues more than ever. My faith was being tested, and my mind was flooded with doubt. As I began to pray in tongues, the doubt left. The Holy Spirit knew exactly how to pray for me. I began to trust God like never before. The Holy Spirit knows what each of his children needs. Will you trust him today to allow him to intercede for you?

Dear Heavenly Father,

I repent of my sins. I ask you for forgiveness. I pray that you strengthen my prayer life and give me a burden of prayer. I need for you to strengthen my tongues. God, your spirit searches my heart and know what the mind of the spirit is. I thank you for allowing the Holy Spirit to make intercession for the saints. I seal this prayer in Jesus mighty name. Amen.

THIRTY ONE

Day Twenty Eight

Today's Scripture for meditation: Romans 11:34 says, "For who hath known the mind of the Lord? or who hath been his counselor?"

Going through life, we often encounter many challenges. We may face certain tests on our jobs, in our relationships, with our health, and so on. Despite the trying times, we still have to hold on to the promises of God. We might find ourselves battling things in the natural or those things that we can visualize. Also, we could be battling things in the spirit which are those things that we can't see with our natural eyes. Throughout the doubt and fear, we have to think about God's goodness.

Who can truly comprehend the things that God wants to do in his children's lives? If we were to ponder on this very thing, we would truly be in awe. This is why it is vital to believe the word of the Lord over all. God will not disappoint you in the end. We may have to suffer at times, yet the reasons why you went through the things you suffered will be revealed later. Who has truly been able to give God advice? God knows what he is doing. Now, allow your soul to rest in Him.

Dear Heavenly Father,

You are a great God. You have extended your grace and mercy upon me many times. Oftentimes, the enemy tries to attack my mind. Lord, bless my thoughts to line up with your word. I pray for increase faith. I cancel any negative thoughts sent by the devil in Jesus' name. God, I know you are all powerful. I refuse to be in unbelief. I want everyone to see my life as a testament to your goodness. Thank you in advance for answering this prayer.

THIRTY TWO

Day Twenty Nine

Today's Scripture for meditation: Romans 12:2 says, "And be not conformed to this world: but be ye transformed by the renewing of your mind, that ye may prove what is that good, and acceptable, and perfect, will of God."

Throughout all the stressors in life, we have to renew our minds on a daily basis with the word of God. I found this practice very helpful. When I was faced with opposition, I would meditate on a scripture that stated the solution to my problem. As a child of God, we can't always approach problems the way a non-believer would. We have to try a different approach, which is God's approach. Renewing our minds results in peace contrarily when the world around us wants to panic.

We can't blend in with this world and do what everyone else is doing. We have to stand out. Our faith in God will make a difference. When people ask us, "How can you remain calm in a crisis?" "Why are you so happy?" or "How are you making it?" we know that we have renewed our minds with the promises of God. We learned over time to think positively. We gained a trust for God through the trials that we endured. We are transformed more into the image of Christ when we take the time to renew our minds on God's word.

Dear Heavenly Father,

I give you praise. I know that your will for my life is good, acceptable, and perfect. I decree that I will not be conformed to this world. I truly want to be transformed into the image of Christ Jesus. I don't want to get in my flesh and do things that aren't pleasing to you. Lord, bless me with peace and patience so I can continue to wait on you. I just want you to be pleased with my life. Lord, favor me this day. Thank you for answering this prayer. Amen.

THIRTY THREE

Day Thirty

Today's Scripture for meditation: Romans 12:16 says, "Be of the same mind one toward another. Mind not high things, but condescend to men of low estate. Be not wise in your own conceits."

We are called to live in peace with one another. Whenever we are in an environment that is full of strife, envy, bitterness, etc., we lose focus. We need to treat others like how we want to be treated. Over time, many people become high-minded and look down upon others. They forget where God has brought them from and become extremely judgmental. Jesus was lowly. He reached out to the people who seemed unimportant. He took the form of a servant.

God is testing our hearts and minds on a daily basis. He is checking to see if we are full of pride. He wants to see if we are willing to get out of our comfort zones sometimes and minister to people from all different socioeconomic classes. Don't cause further division in the body of Christ by being prejudice, religious, and selfish. Be mindful of your brothers and sisters in Christ. Never think that you are better than someone because of their flaws.

Dear Heavenly Father,

I repent of the times where I was high minded and puffed up with pride. I want to remain humble. I want to live in harmony with others. I want to be a peacemaker. I don't want slander, scandals, and discord to be associated with me. I decree that I will have compassion on the lowly. I decree that I will be used as a vessel for your glory. Lord, change my perspective on the important things in life. I just want you to be pleased with my thoughts. Thank you for answering this prayer. In Jesus' name. Amen.

THIRTY FOUR

Day Thirty One

Today's Scripture for meditation: 1 Corinthians 2:16 says, "For who hath known the mind of the Lord, that he may instruct him? But we have the mind of Christ."

The word of the Lord stands final. We often make the mistake and forget this during the pain and suffering. God's counsel will stand regardless of our feelings. The mind of Christ is a powerful thing. This mind is full of faith and power. When we pray to have the mind of Christ, we will find assurance that we will come out victoriously. We will find out through God that we can push back our adversaries. Jesus walked on water, turned water to wine, cleansed the lepers, raised the dead, and more. These may seem like impossible acts.

Yet, when we put on the mind of Christ, we will experience the impossible! We will begin to think how Jesus thought. We will come into another dimension of God's power and begin to duplicate the acts of Jesus Christ and greater on the earth. A mind that is Christ minded is one that is full of tenacity. People who have the mind of Christ will torment the enemy instead of allowing the enemy to torment them. Christ minded saints are ones who walk in authority because they realize the God that they serve is more powerful than the enemy.

Dear Heavenly Father,

I reverence you. I repent of doubt, fear, unbelief, and not always exercising my faith. Jesus is the ultimate example of a man of prayer that was full of the power of God. I want to be a person of prayer and power also. Jesus never allowed the enemy to stop his purpose in life and I refuse to allow the enemy to stop me. I will put on the mind of Christ today. I decree that I will trust God over everything. Thank you for answering my prayers. In Jesus' name. Amen.

THIRTY FIVE

Day Thirty Two

Today's Scripture for meditation: 2 Corinthians 4:4 says, "In whom the god of this world hath blinded the minds of them which believe not, lest the light of the glorious gospel of Christ, who is the image of God, should shine unto them."

We are all commissioned to preach the gospel of Jesus Christ once we are saved. We have loved ones and people who we will cross paths with that need to hear about this great news! Satan has blinded their minds, and they might not believe in Jesus. However, once we plant or water the seeds of the gospel, God may give the increase meaning bring in a harvest of souls for his kingdom. We are mandated to share our faith with others. Make a decision not to be ashamed of the gospel.

The enemy will try to resist us when we go out and minister. However, we need to be full of God's power and mighty people of prayer. There is no soul that is not worth saving in God's eyes. God can save a wicked and perverse generation if they truly repent. Pray for the lost! Pray that you can minister effectively for God's glory! Ask for a burden to win souls for the kingdom of God! The best revenge against the enemy is to snatch back souls out of the darkness and bring them into God's light. People that win souls are considered wise (Proverbs 11:30).

Dear Heavenly Father,

I give you praise. I want to go back to what's truly important, and that's spreading the gospel of Jesus Christ. Many times, I may get busy with the cares of this life and I don't always do what I am mandated to do. I want to be focused and fulfill my call on this earth. Lord, bless me with strategies, word of knowledge, the gift of prophecy, healing, and the other gifts of the spirit so I can win souls for your glory. I pray that you will use me today to minister to someone who needs to hear the good news of the gospel. Thank you for answering this prayer in Jesus' name. Amen.

THIRTY SIX

Day Thirty Three

Today's Scripture for meditation: Ephesians 2:3 says, "Among whom also we all had our conversation in times past in the lusts of our flesh, fulfilling the desires of the flesh and of the mind; and were by nature the children of wrath, even as others."

In this journey, we will be attacked mentally. The enemy will constantly try to remind us of our sinful past. He will try to reconnect you with people and certain atmospheres that is set up to cause you to stumble. Having the right mindset is vital. Yes, you were once living a sinful life, but now you no longer have to. Cast down those demonic thoughts immediately and make a firm stand to not partake in things that are pleasing to the lusts of your flesh. Practicing self-denial is key.

Years ago, I lacked reverence for God, and I was sold out to the ways of the world. That is not who I am today. I am committed to living a consecrated lifestyle before God. I am willing to suffer for the anointing and pay the price to be used by God in a mighty way. I made a stance to go all the way with God. As I renewed my mind and put my focus on God, supernatural favor began to occur in my life. When I was building my credit and trying to get approved for furniture, internet, and television, God supernaturally increased my credit score. This is the power of having a made-up mind and living uprightly before God.

Dear Heavenly Father,

I lift up your name. I want your will to be done in my life. Lord, I am so thankful that I am no longer that sinful person of my past. I am a new person in Jesus Christ. I refuse to be associated with my sinful past. I am looking forward to your great promises and precious intimacy with you. You have done marvelous works all throughout the Bible, and I know for a fact that you can do something great within me. I decree that I will reflect on your promises daily. Thank you for answering this prayer in Jesus' name. Amen.

THIRTY SEVEN

Day Thirty Four

Today's Scripture for meditation: Ephesians 4:17 says, "This I say therefore, and testify in the Lord, that ye henceforth walk not as other Gentiles walk, in the vanity of their mind."

It's crazy how the enemy of our souls knows the bible. When Jesus was tempted in the wilderness, Satan tried to test Jesus with the scriptures. He was presenting the scriptures but behind it was a perverted twist. The enemy will often whisper lies in our minds. He will try to tempt us to serve other gods just like the Gentiles did in the above passage. We can't take the bait and fall into deception. We have to be led by the spirit of truth which is the Holy Spirit.

We have to guard our minds and saturate it with the word of God. We have to meditate on who God is. When the enemy tries to attack my mind, I rebuke it. Then I fight it with the word of God. Every day we have to put God first and make time. The more word we have within us, the more knowledge and revelation we have to combat the enemy with. Remember, the word of God is alive, and it's powerful.

Dear Heavenly Father,

I give you praise. I honor and adore you. Lord, bless me to not fall prey to the spirit of anti-christ and the lies of the enemy. I decree that I will put my mind above and not on the earth. I decree that I will do whatever necessary to die to flesh. I decree that I will be totally committed to following after Christ Jesus. Thank you in advance for answering this prayer. Amen.

THIRTY EIGHT

Day Thirty Five

Today's Scripture for meditation: Ephesians 4:23 says, "And be renewed in the spirit of your mind."

Just as we have to put our old ways to death when we accept Jesus Christ as Lord and Savior, we have to change our thoughts. There is a supernatural exchange that occurs as we make a commitment on a daily basis to yield to the Holy Spirit. The things we used to do when we weren't saved, over time we lose those desires to sin. We make a choice to deny ourselves and put on Jesus Christ while eventually producing fruits of the spirit. As time goes by, our mindset begins to change. The things that used to cause frustration, fear, unbelief will be replaced by faith in God.

Your soul consists of the mind, will, and emotions. The enemy loves to attack our minds with things that are contrary to what God is truly doing. We must be renewed in the spirit of our minds. We have to allow the Holy Spirit to reign in our hearts and minds. When I made a choice to be optimistic and watch the words that I spoke, a turnaround occurred in my life. I have more peace in my life than ever. I am excited to walk out this Christian journey because I know the Lord is guiding me.

Dear Heavenly Father,

I give you honor and glory. I repent of my sins, and I ask that you extend your grace and mercy upon me. Lord, I reverence you. I want to put on Christ daily. I decree that I will take off the old man which includes having the wrong mindset. I decree that I will renew the spirit of my mind which includes having the right attitude. I decree that things are turning around for me. Thank you for answering this prayer. In Jesus' name. Amen.

Day Thirty Six

Today's Scripture for meditation: Philippians 2:2-3 says, "Fulfil ye my joy, that ye be likeminded, having the same love, being of one accord, of one mind. Let nothing be done through strife or vainglory; but in lowliness of mind let each esteem other better than themselves."

There has to be unity in marriages and other God-ordained relationships. Believers in Jesus preach the same gospel, and anything else is heresy. The key point is unity of the doctrine or unity in their belief in Jesus. Just as Apostle Paul asks questions concerning the church of Philippians and their relationship with Christ, we can apply the following scriptures above. Apostle Paul was very happy when the Philippian church was in one accord and their relationship with Jesus was on the right track. How is your relationship with Christ? Does he give you strength, comfort, peace, or the love that you desperately need?

As a result of many life storms, Jesus is the source of everything that I need. I learned to change my thoughts when I felt lonely, and I found a friend in him. I changed the focus of my thoughts from negativity to positivity when I was being persecuted, and I received comfort. I meditated on who God really is, and I received peace when fear tried to overwhelm me. I rested in God's presence, and I received love when I faced rejection. The list continues. I developed unity with the mind of Christ. In other words, we have to think about situations the way Christ thinks about them. When we do this, we win.

Dear Heavenly Father,

I give you praise. I repent of my sins. I want to give you honor with my life. Lord, let the meditations of my heart and mind be acceptable in your sight. I want to have a mind that is in unity with Jesus. I want to remain calm and peaceful in every circumstance because I know you are working things out. I want to grow in my relationship with you. Lord, thanks for your strength, comfort, peace, love, joy, protection, provision, and guidance that you bring to me on a daily basis. I love you in Jesus' name. Amen.

FORTY

Day Thirty Seven

Today's Scripture for meditation: Philippians 2:5 says, "Let this mind be in you, which was also in Christ Jesus."

The mind of Christ is a mind of the supernatural. Jesus had the ability to get results whenever he was faced with a challenge. Like most of us, we are faced with challenges daily. However, when we change our mindset to a mind full of belief, we can see the hand of God move in our situations. A lot of people desire supernatural results in their finances, relationships, and the list goes on. In order to obtain supernatural results, we need to think as Jesus did. His mind allowed him to walk on water, multiply the fish and the bread, and many other miracles.

When I have a challenging circumstance, I have to decree and declare that the same mind that was in Jesus is also in me.

Instead of me doubting God because the clock seems to be ticking. I meditate on all the wonderful things He has already done for me in the past. I pray and say, "Lord, you promised me this, so I know it's already taken care of." After I pray, I rest in his presence, and I don't worry about it anymore. I let it go, and I know by faith that God is working on my behalf. I realize by doing these steps that I am putting on the mind of Christ, a mind that allows me to get supernatural results and a mind of faith.

Dear Heavenly Father,

I magnify you because you are great! I am thankful that you are keeping my mind on a daily basis. I refuse to succumb to negative thinking. I prophesy that I will put on the mind of Christ daily. I don't want to grieve your presence by doubting and not trusting you. I want my thoughts to please you. I decree that I will obtain supernatural results because my thoughts will line up with your word. Thank you for answering this prayer in Jesus matchless name. Amen.

FORTY ONE

Day Thirty Eight

Today's Scriptures for meditation: Philippians 3:15-16 says, "Let us therefore, as many as be perfect, be thus minded: and if in anything ye be otherwise minded, God shall reveal even this unto you. Nevertheless, whereto we have already attained, let us walk by the same rule, let us mind the same thing."

As we follow Jesus Christ, we should be maturing yearly. Every year, we might have some good times and some bad times. We might have some good seasons or bad ones. When we walk with God for a while, we can reflect on who he truly is. We are less likely to fall apart when a trial comes. We will notice that we have become more seasoned and know that God will come through and deliver on his promises. The reason God allows us to go through various trials is to develop our faith and to take us into a higher spiritual dimension in Him.

Initially, when we are faced with a trial, the human side of us or fleshly side wants to panic. This is why it is so vital to be spiritually minded. We might be dying physically, but our spirit man needs to be maturing or getting stronger as time goes on. 2 Corinthians 4:16 says, "For which cause we faint not; but though our outward man perish, yet the inward man is renewed day by day." Each year, I make sure that I step it up or that I do more than last year. I will study, fast, worship, or pray more to ensure that I am growing spiritually. I want to be spiritually mature. I don't want the milk of the word, but I want the meat of the gospel.

Dear Heavenly Father,

I reverence you. You are mighty. I decree that you are bigger than any trial or mountain. You are all powerful. You are stronger than the enemy. I decree that I will not fall apart when times get tough. Instead, I will stand firm in you and experience the miraculous. I decree that trouble will cause me to get stronger in faith and power. I prophesy that I am growing spiritually each year. I rebuke any stagnancy, and I command a supernatural release in my life. Thank you for answering this prayer in Jesus' name. Amen.

FORTY TWO

Day Thirty Nine

Today's Scriptures for meditation: Philippians 4:7-8 says, "And the peace of God, which passeth all understanding, shall keep your hearts and minds through Christ Jesus. Finally, brethren, whatsoever things are true, whatsoever things are honest, whatsoever things are just, whatsoever things are pure, whatsoever things are lovely, whatsoever things are of good report; if there be any virtue, and if there be any praise, think on these things."

The peace that God gives is surreal. It is obtainable as we focus on Jesus regardless of what we are going through. When I was experiencing anxiety, I prayed these two scriptures. I also meditated on it. I am amazed at how much peace I have doing things that I couldn't do years back. Having a Christ-centered mind helped me get the victory in my thought life. The fear had no other choice but to leave because my mind only had room for the gospel.

As we look at verse 8, we can see what kind of things we are to meditate on. Anything contrary to this is a fleshly mind that results in destruction and negativity. God will give you peace when the warfare is very intense. When the devil tells us that we aren't going to make it, we can say we are more than a conqueror (Romans 8:37). When the devil tells us to quit, we can say we can do all things through Christ (Philippians 4:13). We can counteract every lie with the word of God.

Dear Heavenly Father,

I repent of my sins. I have been going around this circle long enough. I am taking back my mind. I decree that everything the enemy stole from me, I will get it back 1000-fold. I decree that I will have what I say. Lord, I want to get lost in your presence. Lord, I am thankful for the peace that you give. I decree Philippians 4:7-8 which says, "And the peace of God, which passeth all understanding, shall keep your hearts and minds through Christ Jesus. Finally, brethren, whatsoever things are true, whatsoever things are honest, whatsoever things are just, whatsoever things are pure, whatsoever things are lovely, whatsoever things are of good report; if there be any virtue, and if there be any praise, think on these things." Thank you for answering this prayer in Jesus' name. Amen.

FORTY THREE

Day Forty

Today's Scripture for meditation: Colossians 1:21 says, "And you, that were sometime alienated and enemies in your mind by wicked works, yet now hath he reconciled."

There was a time when the saints of God mind were full of wickedness. In other words, the leaders we see today weren't always saved. Some of them did some wicked things, but God extended grace to them. They repented and received the gift of salvation. There are also times where some people's minds are so focused on the things of this world; they aren't even concerned with the things of God. I was one of those people. My mind was full of wickedness, and I found myself acting out some of these thoughts. Everything starts in a seed form because it gives root. When something gives root in our minds, it blossoms.

We have to be careful not to allow seeds of wickedness to take root in our minds. Years ago, I was ignorant of the devil's devices and I failed to cover my mind with the word of God. Now, I always pray that every seed the enemy has planted be uprooted in Jesus' name. The enemy is always plotting against us or the children of God. He will try to plant tares or demonic seeds in the night while we are asleep. We have to cover our dream life. We no longer have to be enemies in our minds against God. We can be his friends. Remember, a fleshly mind is hostile towards God (Romans 8:7).

Dear Heavenly Father,

I am so grateful for my deliverance. I want to give you Glory in every area of my life. I want my thoughts to please you. Just because I think about something doesn't mean you are pleased with it or it doesn't mean it's right. I decree that I will cast down those wicked thoughts in Jesus' name. I refuse to have a mind that is an enmity towards God. I don't want to be an enemy towards God but a friend of God. I uproot every demonic seed planted. I plead the blood of Jesus on my mind. Thank you Lord for answering this prayer in Jesus' name. Amen.

FORTY FOUR

Day Forty One

Today's Scripture for meditation: 2 Timothy 1:7 says, "For God hath not given us the spirit of fear; but of power, and of love, and of a sound mind."

God gives us the ability to have good judgment. With the wisdom of God, we can make sound choices in life. We can feel great about the decisions we make in life without having any regrets or sorrows. No matter what the enemy tries to tempt us with, we can have a sound mind and not fall into the temptation. Everything that presents itself in glitter and gold isn't always from God. If we accept what the enemy tries to present to us, there are consequences that we must have to pay. Some of these consequences can cause us to lose everything including our life.

We should pray for a sound mind daily. A mind that is full of self-control and that doesn't mind waiting on God. When we are anxious, we want to rush God and end up getting outside of his will if we aren't careful. Fear has many forms which include anxiousness. Anxiousness is not from God. Rest in God. Believe in God. Have faith in God. Then your mind will be one of power, love, and a mind of good judgment. You will be amazed at the amount of peace in your life.

Dear Heavenly Father,

I give you glory. I am so grateful that you give me wisdom in life so I can make better choices. I am grateful that you constantly order my steps. Lord, I am grateful that you are with me when I feel lonely or afraid. I am grateful that my works in you are not in vain and I will reap the reward of my labor. When I have trouble, I can call on you, and you deliver me. I give you praise for what you are doing and the things that will come to pass. Thank you in Jesus' name. Amen.

FORTY FIVE

Day Forty Two

Today's Scripture for meditation: Titus 1:15 says, "Unto the pure all things are pure: but unto them that are defiled and unbelieving is nothing pure; but even their mind and conscience is defiled."

God is looking for pure vessels where his power can flow through without contamination. Sin contaminates the vessel. Imagine a glass vase. A brand-new vase is squeaky clean without any spots. Over time, when the vase is in use and not washed out properly, it becomes soiled. Sin is like dirty spots that aren't washed in the vase. The vase becomes defiled or contaminated. No matter what beautiful types of flowers that are put in the vase, they will be contaminated because of the impurities and the leftover dirty residues that are there from over time. We have to ensure that our hearts are pure and allow the Lord to cleanse us.

We can't afford to become a rebellious generation where we believe nothing of truth or where our conscience is defiled by sins. We have to make a choice to allow God to flow through a pure vessel by getting rid of all sin in our lives. We can't listen to teaching that contradicts the word of God. Just like a brand-new vase is squeaky clean without any spots or blemishes, we can also become like this when we are washed in the blood of Jesus Christ. In him, all impurities are washed away when we repent of our sins and believe in him. Sin stains, but Jesus can make a crimson red stain as white as wool (Isaiah 1:18).

Dear Heavenly Father,

Lord, I love you with all my heart. I make a decision to live right. I don't want to play any games with you. Lord, place your fear in my heart so I can serve you and walk uprightly. I present my body to you. I present my heart to you. I give you my heart and time. I decree that I will be a vessel of purity before you. I decree that the power of God will flow through this vessel and it will not be defiled by sin. Thank you so much for answering this prayer in Jesus' name. Amen.

FORTY SIX

Day Forty Three

Today's Scripture for meditation: Hebrews 10:16 says, "This is the covenant that I will make with them after those days, saith the Lord, I will put my laws into their hearts, and in their minds will I write them."

God is a God of covenant. He is faithful. He is ready to deliver his people and to fulfill every promise. Just as God was with the prophets of old, so is he with us. He is all knowing, and he delights in the prayers of the righteous. God is ready to establish his covenant with his people. It' is up to us to be knowledgeable about it so we can acquire it. Applied knowledge is power. God will judge his people because he will deal with them by placing his laws in their hearts.

Many times in life, we get distracted by the cares of this world. We need to get back focused. As we get back focused, we can then reflect on the goodness of God as never before. We will realize that he is with us. We will get a revelation of the different covenants and apply them to our lives. When we have the laws of God in our minds, we will be successful. No matter the challenge, God will cause us to arise and conquer all.

Dear Heavenly Father,

I give you honor. I am so thankful that you are a God of covenant. I ask you to establish your covenant with me. I promise to serve you and obey you for the rest of my life. Lord, place your laws in my heart and write them in my mind. I ask you for a fresh anointing today. Thank you for your faithfulness in Jesus' name. Amen.

FORTY SEVEN
Day Forty Four

Today's Scripture for meditation: Hebrews 12:3 says, "For consider him that endured such contradiction of sinners against himself, lest ye be wearied and faint in your minds."

When you want to give up, think about all the things that Jesus endured. Think about everything he had to suffer. He suffered for us. He was rejected, abandoned, persecuted, humiliated, mocked, and so on. However, he stayed faithful until the end and obtained the victory. His natural mind could have been racing with all sort of thoughts, however, since he was a man of faith, his spiritual mind took over. We have to apply the same principles by thinking with our spiritual minds during the darkest hour.

We have to remind ourselves that we are suffering for the glory of God. Also, that God will get the glory out of any negative circumstance. We have to reflect on Jesus and draw our strength from him so we can also stay faithful till the end. We have to stay faithful over every task the Lord places in front of us. The next time you feel discouragement or weariness, think about all the things Jesus suffered for you.

Dear Heavenly Father,

I exalt you. I repent of my sin. I am in awe of your greatness. I am thankful that Jesus suffered for me. I decree that I will make it to the end just as Christ did. Lord, bless me with endurance. I decree that my situation isn't hopeless. I decree that I will obtain the blessings of the Lord in the land of the living. The fact that I am still alive is an indication that God has something great in store for me. Amen.

FORTY EIGHT

Day Forty Five

Today's Scripture for meditation: James 1:8 says, "A double minded man is unstable in all his ways."

A double-minded man is very indecisive. He can never make a decision and stand on it. He will go back and forth. One day he is for something, and the next day, he is against it. The enemy attacks our minds with double-mindedness. One day we believe God and the next day we don't. One day we trust God and the next day we don't. It all comes down to double-mindedness.

A lot of prayers have been hindered due to double-mindedness. Once, the Lord rebuked me. He said, "Why come to me and pray if you will doubt me afterward?" That was a wakeup call for me. I was very unsteady in my faith. I was like a ship being tossed everywhere on the waves of the sea. I immediately repented, and

I vowed never to give up serving Jesus. I went through significant loss, but through it all, God proved his promises. Don't allow double-mindedness to block your blessings.

Dear Heavenly Father,

I repent of all the doubt, doublemindedness, and fear of the unknown. Lord, I need your help. I can't do life without you. I am desperate for you. I command doublemindedness to go in Jesus' name. I decree that I have the mind of Christ on. I prophesy that this is my time to obtain my promises. I prophesy that this is my appointed time. I decree that I will experience consecutive breakthroughs. Thank you for answering this prayer in Jesus' name. Amen.

FORTY NINE

Day Forty Six

Today's Scripture for meditation: James 4:8 says, "Draw nigh to God, and he will draw nigh to you. Cleanse your hands, ye sinners; and purify your hearts, ye double minded.

During the toughest trials, we need to draw close to God. You will be amazed at how He would draw close to you in return. When we seek God with our whole heart, we will find him. I always tell people that the trials will keep you on your knees. This is where my prayer life was birthed. It seemed for a season, the only relief I got was in prayer. The burdens that I carried was enough to make me want to leave this world.

However, God didn't answer those prayers. Instead, he did a great work in me and gave me another chance in life. He gave me another opportunity to serve him, and he began to restore my life. I had to clean up my life and separate myself from sin. Now, I dwell in his presence on a continuous basis. Remember, the trials are opportunities for God to do something great in your life. The trials are opportunities for you to get close to God as never before.

Dear Heavenly Father,

I repent of all my sins. Lord, you said that you are close to the brokenhearted and you bind up their wounds. Lord, heal my heart and make me whole. I decree that I will live right and close the door permanently to sin. Lord, I need you, and I desire more of you. Lord, bless me to get my priorities in life together. I want to draw closer to you. Thank you so much for answering this prayer in Jesus' name. Amen.

FIFTY

Day Forty Seven

Today's Scripture for meditation: 1 Peter 1:13 says, "Wherefore gird up the loins of your mind, be sober, and hope to the end for the grace that is to be brought unto you at the revelation of Jesus Christ."

Some things take time. Many of us want things to happen fast and literally overnight. However, if this was to always happen, we wouldn't have time to prepare and learn from life's experiences. God is preparing us for the waiting season. This is the season where it seems as if nothing is happening or that your prayers are hitting a brick wall in the spirit. We have to prepare our minds for God's best.

We have to prepare our minds for service. Every week, I have to prepare my mind to prophesy. I have to withdraw myself and go somewhere quiet to pray. I meditate on many scriptures and listen quietly to hear what the Holy Spirit is speaking to my heart and mind. I am being prepared for another week of ministry. Preparation takes time. It takes time to pray, study, and meditate. It's in these moments that the revelation is gathered and the instructions for my next task is received.

Dear Heavenly Father,

I am thankful for who you are. You are so majestic and radiant. The splendor of your glory is beyond words. I am thankful for the time of preparation. I am thankful for your knowledge. I decree that I will keep the right mindset when I am waiting for your promises. I decree that I will prepare myself and be ready for whatever season you will have me in. Thank you so much in Jesus' name. Amen.

FIFTY ONE

Day Forty Eight

Today's Scripture for meditation: 1 Peter 4:1 says, "Forasmuch then as Christ hath suffered for us in the flesh, arm yourselves likewise with the same mind: for he that hath suffered in the flesh hath ceased from sin."

We have to protect our minds from the attacks of the enemy. We have to guard it the same way Jesus did. In other words, imitate Christ and fight those wicked thoughts with the word of God. Arming ourselves likewise with the same mind as Christ includes dying to self. We have to put our agendas aside as we pick up God's agenda. Suffering sometimes is part of God's plan. Remember, God chastises those he loves and sometimes we have to go through various tribulations in order to gain compassion to be able to minister effectively to others.

Remind yourself that you are going through the trials for someone else. You are being persecuted for righteousness sake so you are blessed. Reflect on how people don't like the Jesus in you and don't take the persecution personal. Every time I do a video encouraging thousands of people, there is always someone out there who has something negative to say. I learned not to let that bother me because I am just being obedient to my call. God rewards our obedience.

Dear Heavenly Father,

I give you praise. I decree that I will arm myself the same way that Jesus Christ did. I decree that the enemy will not take over my mind! I bind up every spirit of torment in Jesus' name. I loose upon myself the mind of Christ. I decree that I am the righteousness of Christ and I will not be shaken. I decree that I will set the Lord before me because he is a very present help at the time of trouble. Thank you for answering this prayer in Jesus' name. Amen.

FIFTY TWO

Day Forty Nine

Today's Scripture for meditation: Matthew 21:22 says, "And all things, whatsoever ye shall ask in prayer, believing, ye shall receive."

Have you ever prayed about something and received peace about it? Whatever we ask in prayer, if we believe it, then we will receive it. Sometimes God shows us things in the spirit. It's up to us to believe that it will come to pass. Don't get discouraged by the amount of time you may have been waiting. As you wait, begin to activate your faith by showing God that you do believe Him. This is called activating your faith.

I activated my faith in various ways. When I was single, I would set the table for two because I was believing for a spouse. Before I was engaged, I bought a wedding dress. Before I moved into my home, I made prophetic declarations that I would get a house before a certain date and it came to pass. Continue to believe that your prayers are powerful. Believe that God is moving on your behalf and you shall receive your heart's desires.

Dear Heavenly Father,

I honor you. I am so grateful that you are a true living God. I decree that every mountain in my life will be removed and be cast into the sea. I decree that your word in my mouth is powerful and effective. I prophesy that your word is like fire in my mouth and like a rock that breaks the hammer into pieces. I decree that heaven is warring on my behalf. I decree that any resistance will be broken and I will obtain the promises that I am believing for. Thank you for answering this prayer in Jesus' name. Amen.

FIFTY THREE
Day Fifty

Today's Scripture for meditation: Colossians 3:2 says, "Set your affection on things above, not on things on the earth."

Many times, we miss what God wants to do in our lives. We are so distracted by the cares of this world. We are so busy trying to become a friend of the world that we end up becoming enemies of God. We are trying to keep up with the latest trends and fashion that we end up neglecting the things of God. Just because everyone around you is doing something doesn't make it right. If every person in the church starts cursing, does it make it right? Be careful by being a follower. Be a leader. The scripture warns us to set our affections or the things that are most important to you on the things of God.

When we put God in the center of our relationships, businesses, and homes, they will be under His divine counsel. However, if we are so earthly minded and forget God, then we don't qualify for his divine provision and blessings. When we are God-focused, he will take care of us. When I placed my total focus on him, the Lord shows me that he is my sustainer. He vindicates me every time the persecution arises, and I never have to say a word. Be a God pleaser and not a people pleaser.

Dear Heavenly Father,

I repent of not always having the right mindset and giving more attention to things that are grieving to your sight. I don't want to vex you. I want to love you and get to know you more. I decree that my mind will be yielded as an instrument of righteousness. I decree that I will set my affection on things above and not on things on the earth. I uproot any demonic seeds planted in Jesus' name. Thank you for answering this prayer in Jesus' name. Amen.

FIFTY FOUR
Day Fifty One

Today's Scripture for meditation: Proverbs 3:5 says, "Trust in the LORD with all thine heart; and lean not unto thine own understanding."

Whenever we are in the midst of the trials, we have to trust God will all our hearts. We can't even worry about how things will occur and how God will bless us. When I was facing a financial challenge, so many thoughts were ranging through my mind. I felt burden down, and discouragement tried to set in. I had to pray and praise God regardless of how I was feeling. I reminded God of every prophecy that I have ever received, and I went on an extended fast. I was faced with the ultimate trust test which was "Do my actions line up with the words that I am confessing?"

When I realized that I was fully trusting God, I wasn't anxious about anything. I had peace about the situation regardless of how trying the circumstances seemed. I had to let all the worrying go and receive supernatural comfort. I didn't lean into my own understanding or my own carnal mind trying to figure out things that were out of my control. At the right time, God delivered on His promises. It was amazing to see things come to fruition before my very eyes. Rest in God. Trust Him. Watch him move mightily in your life.

Dear Heavenly Father,

You reign! You are high and lifted up! You are so faithful! Your word is true, and you are righteous! God, I make a decision today to cast all my cares upon you. I will focus on you and become a good student of the word. I will spend the time necessary in prayer and devotion to become equipped for every task that you set before me. I am thankful that you choose to order my steps. I am thankful that you will never leave me or forsake me. Thank you for answering this prayer in Jesus' name. Amen.

FIFTY FIVE

Day Fifty Two

Today's Scripture for meditation: 2 Corinthians 10:5 says, "Casting down imaginations, and every high thing that exalteth itself against the knowledge of God, and bringing into captivity every thought to the obedience of Christ;"

Casting down thoughts that are contrary to what God has promised us is one of best strategies against the devil. Whenever we dwell on thoughts such as things pertaining to lust and perversion, those thoughts begin to take root in our minds. The next thing that occurs is that these wicked thoughts will begin to overtake us and then we will begin to act them out. Be careful! Yet, if you cast those thoughts down immediately and rebuke them out loud, it would not take root.

I took the time to meditate on 2 Corinthians 10:5, and it changed my life. The tempter can no longer control my thought life. I suffered from anxiety attacks for 5 years, and daily, the enemy would tell me how he was going to kill me. If I knew what I know now back then, the attacks wouldn't have lasted for 5 years. Don't dwell on ungodly thoughts. Cast them down. Don't allow the enemy to take over your mind. Fight back! Rebuke and renounce those thoughts out loud. Proclaim that your mind is subjective to Jesus Christ!

Dear Heavenly Father,

You are more powerful than any attacks of the enemy. You have given me authority through your son Jesus Christ. I decree that I will walk in that authority and have a mind that is subjective to Christ. I rebuke insanity in Jesus' name. I decree that I have the mind of Christ on today! I will not go crazy and end up in a mental asylum. I decree that the blood of Jesus will saturate my mind and even my thoughts life. I decree 2 Corinthians 10:5 which says, "Casting down imaginations, and every high thing that exalteth itself against the knowledge of God, and bringing into captivity every thought to the obedience of Christ. Thank you for answering this prayer in Jesus' name. Amen.

About The Author

Kimberly Moses started off her ministry as Kimberly Hargraves . She is a highly sought after prophetic voice, Intercessor and a prolific author. There is no doubt that she has a global mandate on her life to serve the nations of the world by spreading the Gospel of JesusChrist. She has a quickly expanding worldwide healing and deliveranceministry. Kimberly Moses wears many hats to fulfill the call God has placed on her life as an entrepreneur over several businesses including her own personal brand Rejoice Essentials which promotes the Gospel of Jesus Christ. This brand includes a magazine and anointing oils. She also serves as a life coach and mentor to many women. She is married to Tron and also the loving mother of two wonderful children. Kimberly has dedicated her life to the work of ministry and to serve others under the call God has placed over her life.

Kimberly currently resides in South Carolina.She is a very anointed woman of God who signs, miracles and wonders follow. The miraculous and incessant testimonies attributed to her ministry are incalculable, with many reporting physical and mental healing, financial breakthroughs, debt cancellations and other favorable outcomes. She is known across the globe as a servant who truly labors on behalf of God's people through intercession. God blessed her to start her ministry to help encourage others. God used her pain to reveal her writing ability and to do his work. God blessed her to write about life experiences and give a message of hope to others with broken hearts.

She is the author of The Following:

"Overcoming Difficult Life Experiences with Scriptures and Prayers"

"Overcoming Emotions with Prayers"

"Daily Prayers That Bring Changes"

"In Right Standing,"

"Obedience Is Key,"

"Prayers That Break The Yoke Of The Enemy: A Book Of Declarations,"

"Prayers That Demolish Demonic Strongholds: A Book Of Declarations,"

"Work Smarter. Not Harder. A Book Of Declarations For The Workforce,"

"Set The Captives Free: A Book Of Deliverance."

"Pray More Challenge"

"Empowering The New Me: Fifty Tips To Becoming A Godly Woman"

"Walk By Faith: A Daily Devotional"

"School Of The Prophets: A Curriculum For Success"

You can find more about Kimberly at

www.prophetessk.org. Follow Kimberly on Facebook at https://www.facebook.com/seerprophetesskimberlyhargraves/.

Follow Kimberly on Twitter and periscope @SeerProphetessK.

Index

A

abomination, 40
affections, 110–11
agreement, 8, 18, 20
anointing, 19
atmospheres, 76

B

battles, 1, 42
believing, 3, 108
blessings, 35, 99, 101
bondage, 7, 30

C

captivity, 60, 115
carnal mind, 63, 113
cast, 9, 31, 45, 59, 76, 109, 113
comfort, 33, 83
conscience, 94–95
covenant, 38, 96–97

D

decree, 8–9, 31, 43, 53, 59, 71, 79, 81, 87, 89, 105, 107, 109, 111, 115
deliverance, 2

E

earth, 38, 75, 79, 111
enemy, 5–8, 11, 13, 49, 59, 67, 73, 75–76, 78–79, 87, 89–92, 115
evil, 58–59

F

faith, 13, 17, 23, 31, 34, 39, 45, 65, 67, 85–87, 100
faithfulness, 45
fasting, 7, 57
flesh, 62–63, 76, 79, 106
forgot, 45, 48

G

glory, 27, 38, 49, 51, 61, 63, 71, 75, 81, 91, 93, 105
God, 4–11, 13–15, 17–23, 25, 27, 29–35, 39–41, 48–51, 58–69, 71–75, 77–80, 88–97, 101–4, 110–11, 113–15
godly life, 52
gospel, 4, 25, 49, 74, 87, 89

H

hearts, 14–15, 24–25, 32, 48–49, 55, 57, 83, 89, 95–97, 102–3
honor, 15, 35, 51, 59, 79, 81, 83
humble, 43, 47, 53, 55, 59, 71

I

idolatry, 45
idols, 48–49
image, 69
intercession, 61

J

journey, 36, 76

K

knowledge, 49, 75, 79, 105

L

leader, 63, 110
Lord, 15, 19–20, 22–23, 25, 27, 29, 34–39, 43–45, 48–49, 52–53, 55–57, 59–61, 77–79, 95–97, 103
love, 33, 47, 54, 83, 92–93, 95, 111
lusts, 76, 114

M

magnify, 19, 27, 29, 45, 53, 57
manifest, 17, 36, 38
meditation, 5, 7, 57, 83
minister, 50, 71, 75, 106
miracles, 17, 84

O

obedience, 107, 115

P

pain, 1, 35
peace, 9, 19, 47, 63, 81, 83, 88–89, 93, 113
power, 11, 13, 18, 22, 29, 37, 87, 92–93, 96
prayer, 7–8, 34–35, 57, 65, 67, 69, 79, 85, 100–102, 107–8, 113
prioritize, 44, 57
promises, 21, 31, 36–38, 45, 69, 77, 97, 101, 105, 109
prophesy, 13, 19, 31, 85, 87, 101, 104, 109
prophet, 36, 43

R

rebuke, 15, 35, 59, 79, 87
renew, 53, 68–69, 81
repent, 29, 31, 43, 45, 57, 59, 63, 65, 71, 73, 81, 83, 99, 101, 103
reprobate mind, 58–59

revelation, 79, 104
righteousness, 9, 61, 107, 111

S

season, 44, 53, 65, 102, 105
sins, 13, 17, 41, 43, 53, 59–60, 63, 65, 81, 83, 89, 95, 99, 103
souls, 4, 14–15, 55, 67, 74–75
strength, 45, 53, 57, 83
supernatural results, 84–85

T

trials, 19, 26, 35, 86–87, 102, 107
trust, 15, 17, 37, 47, 69, 112
truth, 4, 49, 95

U

unbelief, 3, 31, 67, 73
unity, 82–83
uproot, 9, 91, 111

V

vessel, 71, 95
victory, 19, 88
vision, 27, 36

W

wickedness, 6, 90
wisdom, 39, 43, 93
worry, 16–17

Y

yokes, 6

www.ingramcontent.com/pod-product-compliance
Lightning Source LLC
Chambersburg PA
CBHW071516080526
44588CB00011B/1445